Seductive Beauty
of
Great Salt Lake

IMAGES OF A LAKE UNKNOWN

Essays by
Ella Sorensen

Photographs by
John P. George

GIBBS·SMITH
P
PUBLISHER

Salt Lake City

With love to my parents, Charles and
Audrey Dibble, and friends Craig and Jane
ELLA SORENSEN

Dedicated to the memory of my parents, who
gave me life, perseverance, a passion for
excellence, and a love of the natural world.
JOHN P. GEORGE

We gratefully acknowledge the Nature
Conservancy of Utah for their generous
support for this book.

00 99 98 97 5 4 3 2 1

Text copyright © 1997 by Ella Sorensen
Photographs copyright © 1997 by John P. George

This is a Peregrine Smith Book, published by
Gibbs Smith, Publisher
P.O. Box 667
Layton, Utah 84041

Design by J. Scott Knudsen, Park City, Utah

Printed and bound in Hong Kong

Library of Congress Cataloging-in-Publication Data

Sorensen, Ella.
    Seductive beauty of Great Salt Lake: images of a lake
unknown/by Ella Sorensen: photography by John P. George.
        p. cm.
    "A Peregrine Smith book"—T.p. verso.
    ISBN 0-67905-703-3
    1. Great Salt Lake (Utah)—Description and travel.
2. Great Salt Lake (Utah)—Pictorial works. 3. Natural
history—Utah—Great Salt Lake. 4. Natural history—
Utah—Great Salt Lake—Pictorial works. 5. Bird refuges—
Utah—Great Salt Lake. 6. Bird refuges—Utah—Great
Salt Lake—Pictorial works. I. George, John P. II. Title.
F832.G7S67 1997
979.2'42'00222—dc20   95–44989
                                    CIP

Contents

Acknowledgments   6

Photographer's Notes   8

Introduction   9

Brine Fly Enchantment   10

Mistaken Identity   13

Harmony of Herons   14

Shorebird Bonanza   22

A Mirror of Merit   30

Snowy Plovers, A Well-Kept Secret of Great Salt Lake   40

Weaving Cattail Baskets   46

Sacred Worth of Iodine Bush   52

Red Fox Dichotomy   60

The Wind Whistles through Curlew Wings   66

Beauty to Nourish the Soul   70

Seduction   76

Great Salt Lake's Phantom River   80

A Grebe Called Hope   86

A Dalliance with Eternal Flames   90

Acknowledging the Masterpiece

It was not through our toil or labors that the lake was created. It was not our ideas that sprouted and blossomed.

It was not our hand that placed the brine shrimp and the brine fly so abundantly into and upon the water. Nor gave to each the algae that so richly sustains their life.

It was not a song from our lips that set the seasons, the harmony and rhythms to which the wings of birds give heed.

The curves and straight lines that define the island skylines are sculptures by some other, designed.

The waters flow to patterns molded to another's will.

Does not whatever or whomever we believe created the lake, deserve our acknowledgement of the masterpiece? Our appreciation of the magnificent handiwork?

ELLA SORENSEN

Swirling waves, foam and pink-tinted Stansbury Island from Fremont Island's western shore.

Acknowledgments

So many people are part of this book, so abbreviated the space for thanks, that too much appreciated remains unacknowledged.

Much of the information that found paths into my essays has been mined from six deep, rich veins of pure informational gold:

Dr. Ty Harrison gave me the glorious insight that the land can be read by stories plants have to tell. Dr. William H. Behle's lifelong work on the distribution of birds of Utah has been the foundation on which I built my knowledge. Being chosen by him to coauthor a revised checklist of birds in Utah with Dr. Clayton White was one of the highlights of my life. Dr. Don Currey's intellect and knowledge can in an instant turn a bunch of isolated geological facts into a truly awesome wonder. Don Paul, who literally flies with birds of the lake, has shared his knowledge gained from his censuses generously at all times. Guy McCaskie of California, a giant among national bird identification experts, spent enormous amounts of time mentoring me when I was a fledgling birder. Tim Smith has shared with me his insight and the tallest peaks of islands of the lake.

Many answered innumerable questions about the natural world or read some of my essays and made valuable suggestions, including Dr. William Behle, Terry Sadler, Dr. Kimball Harper, Dr. Joseph Jehl, Dr. Tom Lyon, Susan Driggs, Terry Swanson, Brenda Coles, Dr. Kevin Jones, Dr. Don Currey, Dr. Ty Harrison, Justin Dolling, Richard Webster, Paul Lehman.

Through common dreams of conservation projects on Great Salt Lake, the lives of certain individuals have been interwoven with mine. Frank Dunstan, former director of National Audubon Sanctuaries, had the faith to put me in a leadership role and launched me on an untraveled path that has made all the difference. The natural world has a powerful ally in Chris Montague. He moves with grace and ease in every situation. Wayne Martinson has been a steady foundation. Jesse Grantham, Dan Beard, John Kadlec have been part.

Kenn Kaufman first sparked my interest for writing. My associates at the *Salt Lake Tribune* nurtured it. Tom Wharton and Jim Woolf took me as an unconfident beginning writer and built in me confidence to try new things. Mark Knudsen's sensitive illustrations that often accompany my articles are magnets that draw readers. I have always felt the support of Dave Ledford and Jay Shellady.

It is with the deepest heartfelt gratitude that I acknowledge my debt to Dr. Keith Dixon, Steve Hedges, Steve Domino, and Bob Walters, who supported me at pivotal times in life when my ideas were wildly unpopular.

Lake access is exceedingly difficult. To those who so freely allowed access to the lands they owned or managed, I owe some of the richest experiences of my life: Dave Hinckley, Dave Rideout, Bill Kidder, Gordon Miller, and the families of Edward Lincoln Gillmor, Charles F. Gillmor, and Steve Gillmor Jr. Justin Dolling has taken me into the heart of the lake.

Craig Kneedy lives in every essay, so intertwined was our experience, so communal the things we learned. We walked alone together for so long I no longer know what belongs to me and what was gifted from him.

To work with John George is a humbling experience. The loveliness of his photography always haunts me.

I am indebted to Gibbs Smith for believing in this book and to Madge Baird for winnowing out the chaff.

I owe my deepest love and gratitude to my family—my parents, who nurtured my beginnings, and Kristie, Jeremy, Scott, and Richard, who are my bedrock that makes everything else in life worthwhile.

ELLA SORENSEN

The first acknowledgment I make must go to the lake—the great teacher—if one is willing to open one's eyes beyond the normal bounds of what beauty "should be." It was here first, and it will remain long after we are gone—constant but ever changing.

Waiting for the decisive moment or trudging through oozing mud is not conducive to maintaining friendships. Joe Kamenski, a longtime traveling companion and an excellent photographer, provided transportation to Fremont Island as well as patience and a spirit of adventure. The accompaniment of his son, Karl, was a bonus. Our three days on the west bay of Fremont Island were otherworldly, yet less than ten miles from Ogden. Wild storms, rainbows, magnificent sunrises and sunsets, and a return trip to Antelope Island where we were hit by forty-to-fifty mph gale winds will long be remembered. My thanks to the Richards family for granting the necessary access, and to Tim Smith and Jim Fillpot of Great Salt Lake State Park for their assistance.

Ella Sorensen, of course, has always been a source of great knowledge about the lake. As this project matured from wishful chatterings at the kitchen table to the realization that our dreams about the book have come true, we know how much we ourselves have changed because of unwavering determination to remember that the lake is primary, everything else a distant second. We were able to remind each other of that when the vision seemed to drift. Fortunately, our passion for the lake has always remained.

Don Paul and Justin Dolling of the Utah Division of Wildlife Resources provided knowledge and access to the avians who populate the surroundings of the lake. Mike Beal and Karl Oelke befriended me on many trips to the north arm. Mike probably doesn't realize how much his thoughtfulness was appreciated when he provided my son and me with fresh water after our ill-fated attempt to hike out to Gunnison Island with overloaded seventy-pound packs.

Our friends at Masterlab—Steve, Karen, and Jim—have always done a magnificent job at bringing the latent film image to life. Their constructive comments and helpful suggestions have always been appreciated.

Thanks to Madge Baird for her guidance and understanding and to Gibbs Smith for the vision to carry out such a project. It wouldn't have happened without them.

Like other nomadic photographers, I have been fortunate to have the support of my family. John and Jennifer accompanied me on a couple of trips around the lake. Their companionship was appreciated; maybe the lake spirit will one day take hold of them also. They are my link to the future. The encouragement and support of LoWanee can't be overstated, not just for this project, but for my twenty-five years of wilderness wanderings—she has been the source for my photographic passions and inspirations. With love and special thanks!

JOHN P. GEORGE

Photographer's Notes

Having lived quite close to Great Salt Lake (less than five miles as the gull flies) for thirty-five years, much of that time I have thought of it as an abomination to my conditioning on what a beautiful lake should be. It should have white, sandy beaches, not mud flats and salt playas. It should have trees and grass, not pickleweed and iodine bush. It should have fresh water, not water so salty that little can live in it. It should have fish and ducks, not brine shrimp and plovers. It should smell fresh and clean, not putrid and foul.

In 1988, I gave my sister and brother-in-law from Texas the usual tourists' view of the lake at Saltair. Walking that evening on the mud flats left in the aftermath of the mid-'80s flooding was when my attitudes first started to change. Something about that evening was special, in spite of the typical odors. A transformation began to occur, slowly at first. The seduction had begun. My preconceptions about beauty began to change. After all, this is a desert. My visits to Great Salt Lake, lugging a 4x5 camera, began to increase in frequency. Over a hundred of my days have been spent around the lake, not all of them photographically productive, but each one unique to the conditions of that day. I began to learn about the interweaving connection some birds have with the lake; why certain species of salt-tolerant plants were located where they were; about the nature of brine flies.

What a fascinating beauty I began to notice in mud flats, saline flats, pickleweed, shorebirds, brine shrimp, and enchanting desert islands that dominate the horizon. What a treasure I had in my own backyard! Over two thousand images have been made since that evening in 1988, almost a thousand in 4x5 format. The seductress had won, unquestionably. I still don't think Great Salt Lake is a pretty place, but its unique beauty is unsurpassed. The smells are the lake, as are the magnificent sunsets, the salt-tolerant plants, and those birds that make Great Salt Lake their home. Access to many areas of the lake is difficult but not impossible. Prepare mentally and allow the seductress to take hold.

JOHN P. GEORGE

Introduction

There are many misperceptions about Great Salt Lake—words misspoken long ago, then echoed down the canyons of time, bounced so often from generation to generation that the echoes are now considered truth. Inkweed . . . iodine bush . . . snowy plover . . . American avocet . . . marbled godwit . . . eared grebe . . . phalarope. Not exactly household words in the valley of Great Salt Lake. It is our loss, for they are important components of a magnificent, salt-loving ecosystem we have scarcely taken time to know.

Sometimes I think of Great Salt Lake as a lake without a face, without an identity. I ponder, without resolution: What has gone wrong? Why has so much that is unique and beautiful about our salt lake become the object of scorn and derision, been ridiculed or stamped out and replaced with some counterfeit version of what someone thinks the lake should be?

Why do plans for making a freshwater lake proliferate when we have a unique treasure whose ecology is scarcely understood. Why do we continue to focus on creating only freshwater marshes with bulldozers and steam shovels—calling it enhancement and mitigation—and scrape away and destroy unique saline flats and a salt-loving plant ecosystem and the animals that depend on it? Why do we smugly dump our toxins and wastes into the lake, assuring each other through words of the harmlessness and shift the burden of our errors onto those who come after us? Why do we continue to build our human institutions closer and closer, strangling the lake, and then, when the lake rises—as it surely will again—we chant: the lake destroys, the lake destroys, the lake destroys. When will we learn that it is not the lake that destroys, but we who are destroying the lake? The lake reclaims its own. Too many people have talked about what the lake should be and what the lake should do for us, but so very few have ever stopped to listen to what the lake is. Those who do almost invariably fall deeply in love with this shallow lake that speaks a special language.

This is not a book against human development. That is far, far too complex an issue. This book is a plea to go to the lake with an open mind. Our greatest teacher will be the lake itself, and much of what it has to teach us has not been, nor ever can be, captured by the written word. With few people having had access to the lake, and with a value system favoring development, I now watch with abject horror as some of the nicest, well-meaning individuals, agencies, and organizations plan the future of this lake. As I listen to the language and to the spoken words, I tremble for the lake, for it seems many do not have a clue to the unique natural treasures Great Salt Lake holds or what their plans will ultimately destroy. It is time to shed our misperceptions and misspoken words, to peek behind the mask we ourselves have painted that obscures the face of the lake and seek the true identity of Great Salt Lake.

ELLA SORENSEN

Brine Fly Enchantment

When this book was but a fancy, I chatted at my kitchen table with a friend, telling him how I wanted to write a book about the significant little things, not from the human perspective as most books have been written but from the lake's; how I wanted to write about things I have found to be beautiful that have been largely ignored or greatly undervalued.

My friend offered one piece of advice: "Don't, whatever you do, say anything about the brine flies." He didn't want me to ruin a perfectly good book with talk of those pesky, stinky, annoying little things that ruin the lake and that everyone hates.

He was incredulous when I told him I was really quite fond of brine flies. He could not fathom why, and so I told him:

"I find the flies aesthetically pleasing. They never bite. I have rarely had one land on me. In fact, they seldom fly more than a foot off the ground.

"The adults, who live only three to four days, often blow off the water by the trillions, fringing the lake with a ribbon of black. Many a poet has written odes to flocks of shorebirds that twist and wheel and rotate in unison through the sky. But I have experienced the brine fly as well and know it rivals any maneuvering shorebird. I doubt I could step on a brine fly, for each frolicking step I take down, the swarming, fly-covered strand ignites split-second, mini-explosions as thousands of flies blast sideways, opening a bare earth path that I tread with sensual pleasure. Each fly, abruptly displaced, displaces the next fly, sending ripples of movement and soft sound racing down the shoreline.

"And for entertainment," I continued, "the gulls are hilarious when they hunch their backs, lower their heads, and charge down the beach, mouths gaping wide open, bills skimming the ground as they scatter the brine flies from the sand and snap them from the air."

I asked my friend what he thought would happen if we removed the brine fly, as many suggest we ought to do. Without a pause he answered, "The lake would certainly smell a lot better."

How readily and assuredly we unknowingly tinker with this lake. No one I ask seems to know, but some say removing the brine fly would send a stench from decaying algae reeking through the valley with such putridness that we would plead in anguish for the return of the brine fly larvae, which feed on enormous quantities of algae.

And what about the millions of largely ignored shorebirds? Do we really want to remove the brine fly on which many of those shorebirds depend, just as the world's sleeping appreciation for shorebirds stirs, moves, and slowly awakens?

My friend then confessed he had never seen a brine fly and suggested that when I felt like a solitary run down the shore through the brine flies, I consider making it a twosome.

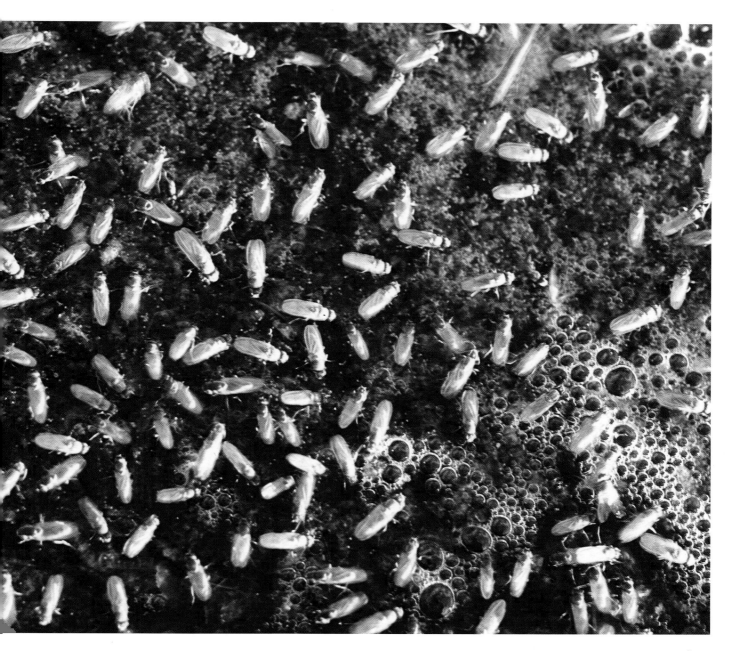

Brine flies.

Brine shrimp.

Mistaken Identity

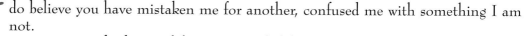

I do believe you have mistaken me for another, confused me with something I am not.

I am not a freshwater lake. I am a salt lake.

I am not as most lakes—a water pause in a downward procession to a lower rung. In millennia past I have been, and perhaps in the future I will be again; but for today, I am the bottom rung. My surface lies over five hundred feet below the overflow valve that controls my maximum depth. Therefore, I am a lake whose levels are unstable and depend on climate. Until you gain control of the vagaries of climate, it is better to allow me space.

Some have said that not a single oasis exists on my shores. But in my entirety, I am an incredibly rich oasis. My waters teem with life. And that life attracts other life forms. I am a fertile stopover for millions of migrating shorebirds, swans, ducks, swallows, grebes, and many other species seeking respite from the surrounding desert. Perhaps you could broaden your restricted definition of oasis to include more than humans and green trees.

Did you come to my shores from places where vegetation flourished lush and green? Is that why my plants are so foreign that you fail to recognize them as plants? My islands and shores have been called sterile wastelands. Fremont Island was originally named Disappointment by early explorers for its "barrenness." But my upland vegetation is desert vegetation, adapted to low rainfall, rich with different shrubs and beautiful flowers; some places even native grasses remain. On my salty shore grow many halophytes, unique plants that find best expression in salty soils.

Do you call my waters dead because you expected fish and found none? An abundance of plants and animals live within and around my briny depths. If not life, what do you call brine shrimp, bacteria, algae, protozoa, brine flies?

So many have called my shorelines disgusting. Some of oolitic sand seem to fit your desires, but many more are wide expanses of shifting mudflats. This valley where I dwell has been the repository of vast accumulations of fine soil particles, pieces of the mountains brought down through the ages. Through wet and dry cycles, with no outlet to the sea, my waters not only restlessly travel and roam back and forth across the surface but also ebb and flow within the spaces between the particles of soil. Even the firmness of a dry mudflat is fickle, instantly turning to a muddy morass with the rain. Until you can remove the soil deposits of many millennia, my outline will remain a blurred boundary of water and earth, constantly changing with time.

But come. All is not lost. There is still time to correct this case of mistaken identity. Time to move beyond the half-truths, untruths, and misspoken words and discover who I am.

No longer should we be strangers living side by side.

Your acquaintance will give to my muteness a voice.

With your acknowledgement, my truth will be known.

For it is in your appreciation that the seeds of my survival lie.

Harmony of Herons

The great blue heron has perfected the pause—it is a master of motionlessness. With stillness that often lasts longer than movement, this heron is often thought of as a silhouette.

The heron's shape is distinctive. When standing erect, most of the four-foot space between head and toes is filled by two skinny legs and a snakelike neck.

When hunting, this solitary bird appears as if rigidly etched on a marsh scene. The heron stands in shallow ponds or along streams, neck folded in a flattened S shape, watching the water, waiting, waiting, waiting, scarcely stirring. When a fish swims near, only then—and with lightning speed—the curved neck straightens, dragged down by a dagger bill, plunging with deadly aim.

When the heron walks, stealth secrets each step from all but the wariest. Slowly, deliberately, a foot rises out of the water, slides forward and reenters with scarcely a ripple.

In early July, desiring to write of herons not from books or memory but from life, I visit a rookery at Farmington Bay Waterfowl Management Area. In a place where flatness reigns, the silhouettes of a dozen blobs high in a row of dead trees appear long before I enter the refuge. Through binoculars, the blobs become large platform nests of interwoven branches. A dozen adult herons stand like sentinels at the nest edges. One or two herons guard most nests, but some are empty. From several nests, tiny baby heron heads poke just above the rim.

Midday is quiet in the heron rookery. Occasionally one of the herons preens or ruffles its feathers. Mostly they rest.

I catch movement in the large middle nest. A female with a stick in her bill leans over the edge, shakes it, then weaves it into the nest's lattice. Halfway between flat and straight up, a ten-foot branch shoots skyward from where she labors. Perched midway stands the male, placidly observing.

She finishes with the stick, then rests. He turns, walks up the branch, and leaps into an abandoned nest. He pokes here, tugs there, and suddenly flaps his wings for balance, returning to the branch. Then like an acrobat on a tightrope, he repeatedly balances his entire gangly frame on one spaghetti leg as he swings the back leg down, around, and past the front one, and his toes clasp the branch. I notice the twig in his bill just as he nears the female, who lifts her bill high, and in one fluent movement they connect and the transfer is made.

Again he watches. The three nestlings rise up, extend their necks and pick at her breast feathers, then jab at each other as they sink back down. She takes her time, experiments, and finally adds the twig to their nest.

Four repetitions of this behavior. Four more sticks to strengthen a nest.

The male then flies off, neck folded back, wings beating slowly and deliberately. He sails in for a landing in a nearby meadow, his descending body trailing his dangling legs, then ambles back and forth across the grasses. He swings his high-held head from side to side. I wonder if he is hunting for voles, as herons sometimes do. But he bends his neck and gathers in his bill a huge branch from the ground and flies back toward his remodeling project. The stick, almost equal to his six-foot wingspan, is agilely maneuvered between the deadwood of the tree. He alights on his branch and starts his downward tightrope walk. She stands still, waiting and watching so that when the moment arrives, the motion flows effortlessly from him to her as if they are notes from the same melody.

As I finally pull away, he has replaced her at the nest and busies himself rearranging, repeatedly pulling a stick from here, tucking it there. She rests in the abandoned nest above, standing on one long leg, the other bent sharply upward at the joint as she scratches the top of her lowered head with her toes.

Within me stirs a recognition—a truth known to herons by instinct. If the heron fills the pause with motion, the fish will seldom be caught. For within the pause, the heron stands still, perched on the edge of the world—watching, and listening, and feeling rhythms of things not of itself. So when the heron moves, it does not blunder forward with movement wasted, mismatched, or unfitting. It enters smoothly into the wider harmony of everything around.

ADAPTED FROM AN ARTICLE PREVIOUSLY PUBLISHED IN THE *SALT LAKE TRIBUNE*.

*Great blue heron
on tree snag.*

*Boulders on eastern
ridge of Stansbury
Island.*

*Salt encrustations
and Stansbury
Island reflections.*

Golden grasses
and Antelope
Island.

Silhouetted bison
and dust clouds,
Antelope Island.

Boulder field,
Buffalo Point,
Antelope Island.

Russian thistle
and mudflats,
White Rock Bay
and Elephant
Head Peak,
Antelope Island.

Shorebird Bonanza

Some would call the pond a cesspool: a smelly, disgusting, mosquito-infested wasteland. But on this chilly September morning, the sky—blue and undimmed by pollution grays—arched westward from the Wasatch peaks to touch the ridge of Antelope Island and stretched one hundred miles north to south. Red, purple, and orange pickleweed encircled the pond with a multicolored border that rivaled the beauty of any autumn canyon. Here, where fresh water spreads shallowly over the saline soil of a playa on the shore of Great Salt Lake, a thousand migrant shorebirds scurried in a frenzy of feeding. Large flocks of dowitchers probed and felt deep in the mud for invertebrates—near-motionless bodies with long, thin bills rhythmically jerking up and down, up and down, up and down like gigantic needles in a sewing machine. Yellowlegs darted about on long, skinny, stiltlike legs, delicately plucking up scattered brine flies that floated upon the surface of the water. Hundreds of least sandpipers, sparrow-small, sprinted around, almost hidden from view among the pickleweed plants. From where did these shorebirds come? Where were they bound? Why had they chosen this pond? And why the impelling, pressing, urgent need to consume food?

Migration, the coming and going of birds as the seasons change, has always intrigued humans.

Migrant shorebirds have developed a unique migration strategy. Huge concentrations of these long-distance migrants often converge on localized food-rich areas. The thousand birds on that small, flooded playa of Great Salt Lake were but a few of the roughly two to five million shorebirds that annually build or replenish fat stores on brine flies, brine shrimp, mosquito and midge larvae, and other invertebrates found in and around the lake. Many shorebirds departing the lake fly thousands of nonstop miles to wintering grounds.

Oh, how we have neglected the shorebirds—one of the grandest wonders of Great Salt Lake. Most of us have never even heard of dowitchers, avocets, stilts, phalaropes, willets, godwits, and dunlins; we can but stumble over their names. Only a few have discovered their secret places and observed their incredible numbers. The thirty-six different species of shorebirds recorded on the lake are as variable as colors of the rainbow.

Some species of shorebirds perform magnificent spectacles, such as the Wilson's phalarope. Every summer, after breeding mostly in the prairies, the vast majority of the world's adult population of phalaropes gather on the waters of Great Salt Lake. On 27 July 1990, 600,000 phalaropes were estimated from aerial photographs. Imagine, approximately 60 percent of the world's adult Wilson phalarope population, on Great Salt Lake, on a single day!

Rafts of these birds can sometimes be seen covering the lake as far as the eye can see. Their heads bob like ping-pong balls and give life to a lake mistakenly called a dead sea. Flocks darken the sky, twisting and rotating like giant amoebas as they move above the surface of the salty lake or commute to freshwater ponds to bathe and drink. It is here

Late summer migration of Wilson's phalaropes on eastern shore.

on Great Salt Lake, feeding on brine shrimp and especially brine flies, that the phalaropes will molt and nearly double their weight before flying three thousand miles nonstop to winter, mainly in Argentina and Bolivia.

Great Salt Lake is the site of one of the largest shorebird concentrations in the world. Each individual bird arrives at the lake with its own history. If a light were lit where each shorebird began its journey, a map of Alaska, Canada, and the northwestern United States would shine as with stars in a night sky. Add a light for each destination and the map would glitter from Utah south through Mexico and Central America to the tip of South America. These shorebirds funnel to the lake like grains in a giant hourglass. Here they feed and fatten on a teeming, concentrated brew of biological energy. Then once again they disperse—a spectacular hemispheric drama.

Utah sits on a front-row seat. Year after year, the play goes on and the actors act, in spite of the near-empty seats.

ADAPTED FROM AN ARTICLE IN THE *SALT LAKE TRIBUNE*.

Black-necked stilt and chick.

Eight-second exposure of wave reflections and feeding American avocets.

*Avocet tracks
etched in mud.*

American avocet.

Great horned owl fledgling.

Nesting long-billed curlew returns to incubate.

Young burrowing owls at den.

*Snowy egret and
cloud reflections.*

A Mirror of Merit

Gunnison Island, nestled deep in the northern arm of Great Salt Lake, is barely 155 acres. It is but a spot on a map. The railroad trestle that split the lake in two—drastically changing the lake's ecology—has, in an odd way, been the salvation of a large pelican colony, for it acts as a buffer against human disturbance.

Up to 18,000 pelicans breed each year on the saddle of the island. The colony is one of the largest in North America. Some years it is the largest. The fish-eating pelicans have sacrificed close foraging areas for the security from predators that an island nesting site provides. Parent birds make flights of many miles to freshwater marshes to fish for themselves and for their nestlings.

In his classic 1940s work on colonial nesting birds of Great Salt Lake, Dr. William H. Behle determined through band returns that many pelicans breeding on Gunnison Island winter deep in mainland Mexico. Reversing the reel of time backwards about 100 pelican generations lands us in the 1500s. It is likely that many Gunnison Island pelicans then wintered in the Valley of Mexico, a geographic setting that bore an uncanny resemblance to today's valley of Great Salt Lake.

There lived the Aztec, or Mexica, as they called themselves. The Mexica recorded their wanderings with paths of bare footprints painted on bark, beaten and softened to paper. Carefully preserved, these sacred pictorial glyphs that tell the Mexicas' story were passed down from generation to generation. So many years ago that time disappears in a mist, the ancient Mexica lived in Aztlan until the sun god Huitzilopochtli told them to leave their homeland. Huitzilopochtli had chosen them to be his people, people of the sun, and he promised to lead them to a new land where they would find their rest, their comfort, and their grandeur. There he promised to make them rulers of the world.

And so those ancient nomadic hunter-gatherers wandered for centuries. Whenever they lingered long enough to settle for a while, Huitzilopochtli urged them onward until at last they entered the Valley of Mexico. This high mountain basin surrounded by forested mountains cradled Lake Texcoco, a great salt lake fed by several large freshwater lakes. This was a rich and fertile oasis in the semiarid landscape.

The Mexica skirmished for decades with other inhabitants before finally retreating onto an island in shallow Lake Texcoco.

There, in 1325, Huitzilopochtli appeared in the guise of an eagle perched on a cactus, devouring a snake; he revealed to his priests that this was the place.

It was a prophecy fulfilled. The wandering Mexica tribe had at last reached their final destination. Immediately they laid a foundation of sod, cut from mud earth, and built a hut of reeds and rushes torn from marsh, dedicating this temple to their god. Tenochtitlan was thus founded.

The Mexica were an industrious people. They used timber felled from the mountains to build their homes and places of business. Stone quarried from the mountains supplied the makings of their palaces. Fine lake sediments were selected to make adobe bricks for their homes. Soon they built three long, straight causeways that linked the island with the mainland. Irrigation systems were perfected for an agricultural-based subsistence.

Moctezuma Ilhuicamina began his reign in 1440, and with the wet cycle a few years later, the human institutions of this enclosed inland basin were inundated with catastrophic flooding. So disastrous was this that Moctezuma himself participated in the building of a great ten-mile, earthen-and-stone dike that prevented future flooding and separated the fresh water from the salty water of Lake Texcoco.

In the mid-1500s, Mexica elders, with the help of a Franciscan priest named Sahagun, recorded almost three hundred essays on animals. The Mexica knew and richly described the birds with which they shared this vast series of lakes and marshes.

Of the pelican, which they said came with the frost, they wrote:

> *It is the ruler, the leader of all the water birds, the ducks. When the various birds come, this is when it comes; it brings them here. . . . This pelican does not nest anywhere in the reeds; it always lives there in the middle of the water, and it is said that it is the heart of the lagoon. . . . It is verily the heart of the water. This pelican also takes with it the different water birds, when it goes. It goes there toward the west, where the sun sets. These water folk consider it as their mirror. For there they see what each is to merit in their profession as water folk.*
> —Florentine Codex
> *Book 11—Earthly Things*
> Fray Bernardino de Sahagun
> University of Utah, 1963

This incredible manuscript reads like a who's who in the bird world of Great Salt Lake. Pelicans, avocets, phalaropes, western and eared grebes, swallows, bitterns, mergansers, teal, cormorants, canvasbacks, et cetera—they were all there. In 1541, Motolinia wrote:

> *There breeds upon the Lake of Mexico a sort of very fine slime and at a certain time of the year when it is the thickest, the Indians gather them with very fine nets until their boats are full. I think particularly that this substance is the bait which brings great multitudes of birds to the Mexican Lagoon. There are so many that in many parts, it looked like a solid lake made up of birds.*

A haunting echo that comes to us from centuries past of another great salt lake.

The biology and human history of Lake Texcoco and Great Salt Lake bear myriad parallels. At times, when reading of Lake Texcoco shortly after the conquest in 1521, when western grebe still called the dawn and the twilight was summoned by rails, when ruddy ducks predicted rain by their flapping wings and the flame-colored swallow could hurl itself into clear water to bathe—it is almost impossible not to lose oneself forward to today on Great Salt Lake.

Culture changed with the conquest, but the driving species remained the same, and the slow-death strangling of a magnificent series of fresh- and saltwater lakes did not alter but continued unabated. Each generation fails to realize that even small changes have horrific cumulative effects. Today, the pelican and all the other birds find the lakes and marshes almost completely gone, replaced by concrete and asphalt. Twenty million people live there now in one of the most polluted cities on earth. Hopefully we will learn from Lake Texcoco's more recent past, and it will not become Great Salt Lake's future. What will time measured in future pelican generations bring?

There is still time to reevaluate where our emphasis on growth is taking us and where it will take those who follow. There is still time for us to rechannel the flow of our high-mountain valley that cradles a great salt lake.

Maybe, just maybe, if humans work with nature, of which we are a part, there will always be brine shrimp for the grebe and brine flies for the phalaropes and plovers.

Perhaps, just perhaps, we can learn the restraint needed to give the pelicans the solitude necessary to continue nesting on Gunnison Island.

> *It is the ruler . . . of all the water birds. . . . It brings them here . . . it is said to be the heart of the lagoon because it lives in the middle . . . it sits waiting . . . it sits looking at them . . . then it calls out, cries out like a crane; it summons the wind. . . . Thereupon the water foams; thereupon the water birds cry out exceedingly. . . . For it is verily the heart of the water . . . This pelican also takes with it the different water birds, when it goes. It goes there toward the west where the sun sets.*
> —SAHAGUN

The heart of our lagoon still beats.

But can the pelican survive us? Perhaps the pelican is for us, as it was once for the Mexica water folk, a mirror of our merit.

Pelican pod on Gunnison Island.

Pelican feeding chick.

*Early dawn over
Gunnison Island
and the Promontory
Range.*

Gull tracks and mudflats.

*California gulls in
flight over
Gunnison Island.*

Sunrise over salt beds on Clyman Bay.

Saline flats surrounding Dolphin Island at dusk.

Snowy Plovers, A Well-Kept Secret of Great Salt Lake

Only a few years have passed since I sat on a sandy knoll with Margy Halpin, a wildlife biologist, and watched a male snowy plover skulking in the pickleweed with two tiny balls of fluff running around on the salt flats on tiny legs. Plover numbers are plummeting everywhere, and we pondered how many breed around Great Salt Lake. Maybe a hundred? Perhaps several hundred? Like so much on the lake, there is little known and nowhere to go for answers except to the lake itself.

"Over there," Peter Paton points. I lazily scan vast saline flats where salt crystals reflect the morning sun. The seductive wiles of brilliant blue waters beckon in the distance. My eyes hasten willingly there but are soon captivated by the early morning purple tints on Antelope Island.

"You're too far out," chides Peter. "It's closer, there in the shadow of the iodine bush." The snowy plover stands still. The tiny shorebird, barely six inches long, weighs no more than a medium-sized chicken egg. The sandy brown coloration above and snowy white below perfectly blends bird and background. The plover scurries across the saline flats, black legs blurring with brisk locomotion. A visual hunter on a quest for brine flies, it stops, searches, sees, then pursues. Stop and go. Stop and go. It moves with the abruptness of Morse code.

Peter Paton, a rugged outdoorsman who skis, kayaks, and backpacks, is completing his fourth year of doctoral study on the snowy plover. Recently he has slowed down. The dawn-to-dusk marathons have shrunk to ten-hour days. And he even takes weekends off—sometimes. With scopes slung over their shoulders and notebooks stuffed in pockets, he and his assistant, Craig Kneedy, trudge sometimes ten miles a day through mud, observing, banding, and recording.

Paton estimates 10,000 plovers breed on the saline flats around Great Salt Lake, the largest concentration in North America. In other western states with sizable plover numbers—California, Oregon, Nevada—Paton estimates there are only 8,000 combined. The Pacific Coast population has so drastically declined that it is now listed as threatened.

Snowy plovers are migrants in Utah; the earliest arrive in mid-March. Nesting starts in mid-April. The nest, a simple scrape in the sand, usually contains a clutch of three eggs. Prime nesting habitat has little vegetation, but the birds prefer some structure such as a dead greasewood plant, a few rocks, or a pickleweed plant. While young songbirds such as robins remain weeks in the nest, snowy plover chicks are off and running a few hours after hatching.

Snowy plovers practice serial polyandry. Male and female share incubation duties, but two to five days post-hatching, the female splits, leaving the male behind to care for the chicks for about a month, until they learn to fly. Off she goes, often many miles away, to find a new mate and initiate another clutch.

During his four-year study, Paton has banded 544 birds, each with a distinct color combination that allows individual recognition. The plovers tend to move around from year to year, undoubtedly in response to thousands of years of experience with an ever-shifting lake.

Once it was thought that Utah birds joined other plovers wintering along the California coast. But armies of observers studying those plovers have yet to find a single bird banded in Utah.

In four trips in search of the wintering grounds, Paton has discovered two banded birds, both at the northern tip of the Gulf of California near the mouth of the Colorado River. Others have sighted a banded bird halfway down the Baja Peninsula and another at the peninsula's farthest tip. Paton suspects that most Utah birds winter in the northern portion of the Gulf of California, and that is where he will migrate himself once again this winter.

I thank Peter for sharing his information, apologizing for keeping him from his research.

"What good is all the research in the world," he responds, "if it sits collecting dust on some library shelf? It is equally important to talk of the plovers, a well-kept secret of Great Salt Lake."

Peter is right. Without awareness, there will never be appreciation.

Previously published in the *Salt Lake Tribune*.

Snowy plover and camouflaged eggs.

Bleached skeleton
and cheat grass,
Little Gillespies.

Pickleweed,
Layton wetlands.

*Salt patterns and
Hogup Mountains.*

Winter blues,
western shore of
Stansbury Island.

Weaving Cattail Baskets

A woman stood on the edge with a cattail poking out of her hair—a cattail she stuck behind her ear in a renegade moment of pleasure, for the task of the day was not adornment but gathering the broad leaves of the cattail plant to weave into a basket.

Her arms so overflowed with her labor that those passing in front could not see her face—only that single cattail sticking up. She found if she twisted her load just right, she could line her eyes with spaces between cattail leaves and peer out to watch stunned faces pass by. This amused her and helped pass the time as she waited for her daughter.

But soon bored, for she was the product of a culture that did not wait well, she turned her back to the northwest wind, away from the grassy edge, and looked longingly back at the wildness she had just abandoned. Suddenly a nearly overpowering force she did not understand swirled turbulently inside her, urging her to cast off her load and scream out to her daughter to come back so they could retreat into the marsh and pick cattails together once again. It was not the cattail picking she yearned to relive but the intense feeling of unity and harmony that felt so right between mother, daughter, and earth.

I shoved the bundle of cattails into the backseat after my daughter Kristie pulled her car to the curb. I was helping Kristie with a college wilderness-class assignment to make a survival aid from material gathered in the wild.

The task proved troublesome, and she agonized for weeks until one evening, as she discouragedly sat on the living-room floor discarding book after book, she turned a page and brightened: *I'll weave a basket from cattail leaves.* And as she planned her project, her mother was woven into her scheme.

I knew of a place not far away where cattails grew next to a road. We parked and wandered over soil that, through the ages, has been relentlessly veiled and unveiled by a briny, watery drape of a restless lake.

Archaeological and geological records confirm that most of the thousands of years humans have been on the scene, the lake's liquid saltwater drape has been drawn at this spot and the earth unsheathed. Through the millennia, the Jordan River, meeting the lake by a course different and lost to most today, flowed over this spot in spring, submerging the salty soil in fresh water.

Here, where the ground dips below the water table and water runs fresh, cattails have grown for a long, long time.

I came grumpy, far too busy to be here while my daughter picked cattails in a marsh. Only because of a promise extracted was I even here at all. I walked over to a nearby sod strip laid beside a busy street and leaned against a tree to study.

But instead, I watched my daughter bending low to pull and jerk, freeing last season's withered, tan cattail leaves from an ungreened marsh of early spring. The book with all its ponderously important words slipped from my mind and fell to the grass.

Discomforted and uneasy with a Norway Spruce trunk pricking my back while my daughter labored alone in a marsh, I felt empty, alone, like I didn't belong.

When Kristie's arm beckoned, how easily I stepped over the edge to the wild and moved lightly to her side.

I pulled and twisted and jerked. I stashed withered leaves under my arm as I joyously gathered cattails with my daughter in a marsh.

We are the sun.

We are the wind.

We are the slate gray mud.

In a moment of whimsy and unabated glee, I snapped a stem and stuck it behind my ear, then snapped another, ruffling the seed head to free the seeds to go dancing away with the wind. The disbursing seeds also went into our eyes and on our clothes and in the water and on the ground, for nature, in planning the cattail, stuffs thousands of seeds into each mature seed head.

Turning, my daughter echoed traditions that my mother once echoed to me: "Oh, Mom, don't be so silly; time is short. You need to get back to work."

But, I told her, forget what I taught you; strands of culture sometimes go awry. Let me tell you what I am now feeling. Something is missing from our lives. I know my words are stumbling—it is so very hard to explain. You and I need more shared moments of pleasure, but what I feel is deeper and more profound. A oneness. A singleness. An undividedness. A sense of coming home. A sense of being home. I have felt many emotions, but this is so unique. Something new and wonderful. Something my traditions have not defined. A forceful bond pulling me with you back to the wildness to which we both belong. Our tradition may tell us we are separate, but we are not! We are part of it all. Think of all the generations before us who came to this very place. Daughters bonding to mothers, weaving traditions of value in the marsh. I just felt the force of that invisible link. I shudder now, knowing how very much you and I have lost.

"Oh, Mom," she reechoed, "I don't have time for this foolishness. The class starts in hours. Let's go home and get this thing done. Here, take my bundle of cattail leaves; I'll get the car and meet you at the curb."

At home, Kristie easily wove ten cattail leaves into a square with twenty radiating spokes.

"Mom," she called, "come help me, quickly. The book's instructions are becoming unclear." I helped her loop a single, long, cattail leaf around a corner spoke to make a pair of weavers that were to be twisted alternately. And when each cattail weaver had played itself out, another was to be added so that a new weaver could continue on.

The next time she called out, it was a bloodcurdling shriek. While the illustration pictured a basket that sloped gently, hers veered abruptly straight up.

I gently closed the book. Wisdom from and for a different place.

Sometimes in life, I told her, when things no longer feel right, there comes a time for parting from what others say must be. The book does not hold the weavers. The cattails are in your hands. Have the courage and faith to let your fingers guide the tension, creating what to them feels right. And let what will be . . . be.

She wove then her basket in confidence, her fingers humming with tunes of their own. She effervesced with enthusiasm over a creation whose pattern had never been cast. And with every successive cattail twist grew the promise of hope as the emerging shape was formed by the rightness in each moment's feel.

A woman stood on the gutter with a cattail poking out of her hair. She knew she was not the first mother to bring her daughter gathering in this marsh. She also knew she would be the last.

Plans were already in motion, and soon the asphalt carpet would roll west, uncontested across this wild, wild land. She was saddened, for she had watched this happen time and time again with little, if any, opposition.

Then something inside her rebelled, and in her mind she made a decision: she plucked two long cattail leaves from out of her heart, touched each to her lips, and then held them to her bosom and wept. Sometimes in life, when things no longer feel right, there comes a time for parting from what others say must be. Hopeful fingers caressed the first leaf as she took the narrow end, overlaid the current weaver of the unfinished basket, and slowly wove in a new weaver. Then she took the second leaf, overlaid the second current weaver of the unfinished basket, and slowly wove in another new weaver. And each time she needed to add a new weaver, she plucked it with hope from her heart. Today she is still weaving and wondering how the basket will turn out.

Frost-tinted cattails.

Skeletal remains and Antelope Island.

Limestone outcroppings and Fremont Island from Promontory Point.

Russian thistle
and mudflats,
Sally Mountain in
Lakeside Range.

Sacred Worth of Iodine Bush

Scattered about the salty shores of Great Salt Lake and up into its saline playas grows a salt-tolerant plant called iodine bush. Scientists call it *Allenrolfea*. Sometimes iodine bush dominates the landscape, dotting large expanses. Sometimes a single isolated plant waves like an ensign atop a little wind-created hummock on the sweeping salt flats.

Its leaves—long strands of segmented ovals strung by nature like beads of a necklace—give iodine bush the appearance of a vigorous, green-growing plant of only stems. Fingers that crush and pop those succulent, stemlike leaves are moistened with juice, color-coded by season. Summer green. Autumn gold. Tongues that lick those coated fingers taste the bitter saltiness that gives the plant its name.

Few of us, who are the latest of many to call this valley home, can distinguish iodine bush from other plants. Many before us could. Almost the entire expanse of time that humans have dwelt in proximity to the lake, iodine bush has been a VIP—a Very Important Plant.

Iodine bush provided subsistence to many who came before us, who lived in caves and knew the seasons of the lake far better than we. In Hogup Cave, just west of the lake, regular but periodic human occupation began about 6400 B.C. In the span of about 8,000 years, as the debris from daily living fell, the cave floor inched slowly upward until it stood eleven to fourteen feet above bedrock. Botanists and archaeologists, working backward in time, sifting downward through thousands of years of cave fill, identified iodine bush chaff, stems, and branches as the commonest plant product in most of the sixteen distinct time layers. Harvest was in the fall.

September 1994, I camp on a mountain slope near the entrance of Hogup Cave. Throughout the night, the landscape is severed distinctly into a zone of darkness and a zone of lightness. The black mountain shape silhouettes starkly against sky brightly illuminated by a full moon. In a peculiar segregation, the expansive salt flats below belong not to the dark earth zone but are claimed by luminous reflection into the radiant realm of light. Gradually the two-toned night departs, chased away by the intensifying of the soft, subtle light of dawn. Looking west, I think backwards and wonder:

How many times in 8,000 years did someone linger here near the cave entrance and feel on their face the cool autumn breeze against the warm sun? How many eyes have gazed below at wide expanses of salt flats and watched the dawn play purple in succession across the multi-distanced mountain ranges? How many hearts were lifted and gladdened as light from a rising sun cast changing iodine bush shadows, painting exquisite salt-flat compositions of shifting tint and hue, texture and shape? How many footsteps of people like you and me descended rocky shadscale and black sage-dotted slopes to mix footprints on saline flats with those of sage sparrows and pronghorn? Intermittently but continuously through the millennia, many backs bent to snap woody branches from this low-growing perennial shrub before ascending with loads back home again. How many hands have

Storm clouds
from inside
Hogup Cave.

threshed and winnowed in the wind, hurling chaff to fly with the air, leaving behind thousands of tiny, nutritious, brown seeds?

The limestone outcrops, which define the mountain ridges and span the hollow space of the cave, formed beneath the waters of some long-ago sea. Now the limestone outcrops tower above a desert. This spot has known great change.

Today in Hogup Cave, four ten-inch stalactites grow slowly from the limestone roof. Each drip, a beat of time. Each lengthening, a measure of change.

The time since humans first discovered the cave is short time, and changes are subtle. A little more of the mountain has become part of the salt flats. The shrubs are the same, but the ground cover has added aliens such as cheat grass and halogeton.

Iodine bush still dominates the salt flats in a narrow band between land that climbs on one side and salt concentration that climbs on the other.

Iodine bush is a halophyte, a salt-tolerant plant, a part of a whole, grand, salt-loving ecosystem magnificently adapted to high-salt concentration. For thousands of years, humans moved in rhythm with that ecosystem.

Today among myriad words written of the lake, scarce is even the whisper of halophytes, these marvels of existence in harsh, harsh places. Words, if we find any at all, more often than not insult: worthless, noxious, barren, sterile, disappointing. . . .

Halophytes are true plants of a briny lake shore, integral essence of a salty place. Since iodine bush no longer lies in the realm of human usefulness, it has fallen into obscurity.

Today iodine bush lies within the realm of beauty, a beauty of existence and shared connectedness. Iodine bush stature will rise again in human eyes when we finally acknowledge that wild natural beauty and intrinsic value exist in everything that is.

Greening iodine bush, Bonneville Salt Flats and Silver Island Mountains.

Salt-encrusted
bushes and
southern tip of
Hogup
Mountains.

Geometrical designs of salt flat, northwest shore.

Lichen-covered
outcroppings,
Grassy Mountains
and Lakeside
Range.

Lichens,
limestone and
grassy slopes,
Lakeside
Mountains.

Red Fox Dichotomy

How magnificently grand! Spectacular and graceful!

The red fox gallops effortlessly across the frozen shores of Great Salt Lake, its reddish fur adding a streak of moving warmth to the icy chill of winter whiteness. Its long, bushy tail follows, floating straight behind.

The red fox slows to a halt. The head turns and the eyes meet mine. Ears erect, body tense, it watches. It watches me. The thrill is ever electric and stimulating each time I see one.

Today fox tracks crisscross the eastern shores of Great Salt Lake wherever there is snow or mud for record keeping. Rare is the day spent when my path does not walk beside or intersect many footprint trails. There are many foxes and many fox tracks where only a few decades ago there were none.

The red fox prospers and continues to expand its territory into new areas. The wetlands of Great Salt Lake is one of those new areas. The red fox is highly adaptable. Not only a skillful, opportunistic hunter of small animals such as rodents, rabbits, and insects, it also scavenges effectively.

No one knows for certain when red fox appeared in lake wetlands. An average date based on opinions from many who have long histories on the shores of Great Salt Lake places the fox's first appearance somewhere around the middle of the 1960s. When, why, from where—red fox's arrival may often be debated, but there seems to be consensus that when the lake rose in the 1980s, the population exploded along the east side of Great Salt Lake and remains high today. The fox moved as a newcomer into a territory long occupied by others.

There are many dilemmas on Great Salt Lake. Every change brings gain and loss. Every change benefits some species to the detriment of others. Everything is connected. We cannot help one without harming some other.

Short-eared owls fly on broad, rounded wings like giant moths, with wing beats so slow I sometimes wonder why they do not fall out of the sky. In the 1970s, rare was my dawn or twilight visit without seeing short-eared owls hunting over the wetlands. Now when I visit, I rarely see one. Some say, with accuracy, that short-eared owl populations are cyclic. But as years tick by, when do we stop waiting for the upturn and concede that a population has crashed?

Short-eared owls are not alone. Long-billed curlew populations have crashed. Nesting ducks, according to refuge managers, have been hit hard. The toll on snowy plovers, according to researchers, has been enormous.

Studies have shown that birds present a most difficult hunting challenge for red foxes. Exceptions are ground-nesting birds in the breeding season. For obvious reasons, birds of Great Salt Lake wetlands do not nest in trees or on cliffs. Most nest on or near the ground. Incubating adults, eggs, and young are extremely vulnerable to mammalian predation.

Raccoons, skunks, habitat loss, and human disturbance have undoubtedly contributed to the large decrease in many bird populations, but many wildlife biologists strongly suspect that the appearance of the red fox in an area where the birds have developed little defense has played a most significant role.

Some say let nature take its course. Predator and prey balance each other. If prey decrease, then predators decrease.

Oh, were it only so simple. Humans have thrown the system out of balance. The fox population in the valley of Great Salt Lake is not dependent upon Great Salt Lake bird populations. When this food source decreases, populations of the adaptive fox are not limited, for they can turn to other food sources in adjacent areas. And there is always our garbage to scavenge on. This does not seem to be decreasing.

Once, the nesting birds of Great Salt Lake were protected by marshy barriers. Many have now been drained or filled. Every road or dike that is built opens a new corridor for mammalian predators to enter the heart of the wetlands and decimate whole populations.

Red fox presence in Great Salt Lake wetlands is, for me, a dilemma—a web woven of strands of uncertain feelings into an unsettling pattern of ideas that are in discord. Wildness dwells in the fox. I admire its adaptiveness and alertness, its reddish fur and bushy, white-tipped tail. If we massacre the fox, are we not interfering cultivators directing the harvest to our own choice, exterminators of the very wildness we claim to revere? But can we stand aside and watch the decimation of populations of other species when the cause was germinated in our own actions.

I love owls and curlews.

I love red fox.

I have no answers. Only the pleasure of new acquaintance with a magnificently beautiful creature, mingled with sadness of a profound sense of loss . . .

ADAPTED FROM AN ARTICLE IN THE *SALT LAKE TRIBUNE*.

Desert kit fox at burrowing owl's den.

Setting moon over Stansbury Island.

Female northern harrier and nestlings.

*Skeletal greasewood
mixed with autumn
plants, Stansbury
Island.*

*Golden grass-
covered slopes and
outcroppings on
Fremont Island,
Antelope Island in
distance.*

The Wind Whistles through Curlew Wings

I don't recall ever being so miserable. I am absolutely, incontestably wretched. The solitary thought racing through my mind sounds like a stuck needle on an old phonograph: I don't want to be here, I don't want to be here, I DON'T WANT TO BE HERE, I DON'T WANT TO BE HERE!

Not a whit of a breeze fans the air.

Not even a single tree to shade from a sweltering sun. I swear the sun rays are in a conspiracy. Every ray for twenty feet around either hits me directly or bounces off a salt crystal to bombard me on the rebound. Sweat soaks my hair. Sweat drenches my skin. When dust migrates with sweat into my eyes, I squeeze my eyelids tightly and wait for tears to lessen the smart.

Scores of deerflies, swirling like a halo, accompany me through the grass. Two fingers and a thumb, stiff and swollen double-sized, sting painfully from their bites. The bloodied gash from a greasewood spike running jagged across my arm matches nearly identically the one running down my leg, added when I fell climbing over a barbwire fence.

My socks, black this morning, are now tan porcupines, so many cheat grass seed heads protrude. On the inside, needle-sharp spikes gouge and welt my skin. I drop to the salt playa, rip off the offending socks, succumbing to the call of the itch.

Sitting here amidst all this misery, I take pause to record a list of conditions that have little human appeal. If I write only of beauty, my words would be incomplete. I have spent many a day on the lake or its salty shores that rate minus numbers on the human-comfort scale. Brutal, uncongenial, inhospitable days that bludgeon both human body and soul.

The faint stirring of a headache reminds me I have foolishly lingered and baked too long. As my body rises, my chin drops low and my feet stir dust from the salty earth. I slowly start scuffling along.

I hear it soft behind me, an approaching echo of some faraway mournful cry.

Curleeee, curleeee.

I wait till it is right above me—flying high and wild and free—to lift my face into a blue, blue sky and see.

Curleeee, curleeee, curleeee, more strident and repetitious now. It molds those cinnamon wings, so fluid when it flies, into stiffened, inflexible arches that vibrate and quiver as it sails about and calls.

Curleeee, curleeee.

It flies about me in circles, then flutters downward, descending to the ground. As side to side it shifts its head, the gigantically long bill thrashes along like a sickle. Each black eye gives the curlew a different view of me and helps it define how far apart we stand.

Upward again, on wings it is sky-bound once more to sound its cry and circle and circle again.

Abruptly all is silent. I look and find a silent dive bomber with accelerating wings heading straight toward me. Lower and lower, eyes to eyes, nose to beak, till skimming three feet from the ground, it passes slightly to my right. With a sharp spread of flight feathers braking the speed, it fearsomely shrieks and veers up just behind me.

To rise and circle again.

Curleeee, curleeee, curleeee.

More than a mile now, I have shared with this curlew earthly time and place. Again and again it zooms suddenly and sharply toward me, closer and closer. It startles me only when I miss its hushed descent and detect its nearness first by that sudden feather brake and bloodcurdling scream. Each time, as the curlew grows bolder, the wind whistle loudens in its wings. The distance I have traveled has taken me far from any nest or chicks it may have hidden in the grass. This curlew just won't give up until it is certain I am chased away.

Oh curlew, I ask, why waste the energy you need to feed your chicks? Go back and protect them from threats that you can. Your antics have no effect against humans. Save it for the fox, skunk, or raccoon. Protection from humans is beyond your control. People must learn respect and restraint from within.

It left me then. And in midday silence, I finally reached my car. I turned slowly back and there it stood, perched far away along the salty shoreline, silhouetted against the blues of a great salt lake. Still trying to protect its home, it stood silently watching me.

If only the curlew had a human voice, perhaps the words would be:

Too many humans come here to my home. Declaring it unsuitable, they complain: This is a place of stinks, a land of noxious bugs and barren flats and water too salty for worth. A place where disappointment dwells. There is nothing to do for entertainment, and no place to buy souvenirs or cold drinks. We need to fix this awful place with green grass, shade trees, and cement. Remodel it into a pleasant place. There is no profit if humans are rebuffed.

But this place you enter is not vacant land nor is it a dead sea.

When you enter, leave behind the arrogant judgment that human comfort is a major standard of worth. Snap a clothespin on your nose if that is what it takes to open your mind. This land has already been written and seeks not your revision.

When you come, come on my terms, as an appreciative and respectful guest. The changes you bring to conditions you deplore are the ruin of my habitat. My survival depends on your restraint. My home belongs not in the human but in the curlew comfort zone.

*Foxtail barley on
Bridger Bay.*

Beauty to Nourish the Soul

Most halophytes—plants that tolerate growth in salty soil—are considered hardy and tough because they can grow in such harsh places.

The truth has a slightly different twist. Most halophytes are able to grow in many places, but are so fragile they simply cannot compete. As soon as fresh water leaches some of the salt surrounding their shallow root system, roots of other plants that cannot tolerate the high salt concentration quickly invade and crowd out the halophytes. Halophytes exist not because they are hardy but because they have evolved wonderful adaptations to handle high salt concentrations and can grow where other plants cannot.

I stumbled across this interesting truth one chilly November afternoon on the salty shores of Great Salt Lake. Snow dusting the little hummocks of the saline plains looked like fluffy white clouds fallen from the sky. Plants wore winter colors: varying shades of pickleweed gray and bulrush tan.

As I sift back through my many times on the lake, that afternoon stands without competition as my most woeful and mournful memory. I had just walked those saline plains with a biologist teaching me the plants. When we came to some alkali bulrush growing in a brackish seep, he tenderly threshed the seedpod and sprinkled tiny brown seeds, a favorite food of ducks, into my hands. It was he who first explained to me that alkali bulrush, a halophyte, can grow many places but is quickly displaced by other plants such as cattails when the soil is leached of its saltiness by fresh water.

Later that afternoon, I walked alone along a favorite path winding through a landscape eloquently arrayed with the skeletal patterns of late fall's withered halophytic plants. My mind was troubled and disallowed its beauty entrance, wandering instead to the relentless assault our burgeoning population creates on the other animals and plants that share our world. Scene after changing scene came to mind. Wild places I had grown to love and then watched in horror as they were ripped apart. Rows of giant trees pushed on their sides by bulldozers, roots instead of branches gaping at the air. Twisted piles of dying, rotting grass, the earth scraped bare nearby. Water oozing from the sides of freshly dug trenches whose goal was to exsanguinate wetlands. Piles of dirt smothering former wetlands. Gouges and tears turning places I loved into devastated battle scenes. Knowing all the while that the birds and other animals and plants with which I had gained familiarity and who found home in those places, never would again. I kept looking at the various halophytes and walking faster and faster, trying to escape the increasing turbulent emotion and thoughts threatening to dishevel my mind.

My sight and thoughts twirled together like partners in an erratic dance of accelerating tempo. I looked and saw inkweed and thought how like wild places. I tried to stop my thoughts. Pickleweed I saw, how fragile those wild places. How vulnerable and unprotected. All halophytes I glimpsed, so wild and fragile they cannot compete. Like halophytes, wild places will always lose, crowded out, displaced. Faster and faster I ran. Faster and faster came the scenes. Till finally, when I could run no further, I dropped in exhaustion to my knees, laid my head to the ground, and wept.

Never have I felt such intense emotional suffering. Never have I felt such remorse for the wanton destruction of other life-forms by my own. That day, the fragile halophytes merged to become the fragile wild places on earth. Wild places so delicate, with the competition so fierce and always lurking, just waiting for the opportunity to invade. Wild places cannot compete; they only exist until they are displaced by our greed for profit, our desire for unrestrained recreation, and our constant need to alter to forms some find more pleasing. Are they doomed? I wept long and bitterly for all the wild places I have personally known and lost because they could not compete with "progress."

I languished in agony, in the tortured, unbearable pain known to all who have suffered great and intimate loss. My soul so intertwined with grief, it could but torment all strength from my body; my vision so narrowed by pain and sorrow, it could but dim everything to darkness around me.

I wandered back in time, massaging each casualty, crushed anew by the weight of each forfeiture. Remembering. Feeling again each wild loss. Knowing we change *wild*'s definition as our tentacles strangle its life.

Suddenly my thoughts focused on the words of an old friend. In memory, his voice came thundering at me with the same fury and contempt it had so many years ago at my first site where humans were destroying the wild I loved.

GO AWAY! My silenced voice screamed at him. I did not want to listen to you then. I do not want to listen now. I pulled my encasing shell of sorrow and pain tighter, trying to reflect his words of treason and surrender back to the place and time I had first rejected them.

This time, his voice found a fissure, a crack from repeated assaults. His words hurled through my shell like bruising stones.

"*You weep too much. You wallow in sorrow. What are you going to do, devote your life to anger and mourning? You can't stop this. Nobody can.*

"*You think I am a stranger to grief. I have loved this place longer than you, and my lengthy life has seen far more destruction.*

"*Fight your battle. The world needs respect for the wild. But remember, while without water we die, with too much we drown.*

"*I am an old man. I have been successful in the ways of this world. I have fought and lost many a battle for preservation. Won, only temporarily, a few. I do not know how many years remain for me. Whatever I have left, I have cast to the winds of pleasure. Now wherever the winds of wild beauty blow, they lift my soul and buoy my spirit and drag this hobbled, tired old body along.*

"*Now wipe your tears. You are lucky. Be thankful. You lived at a time and had the means to be part of the magnificent beauties of this place.*

"*Drink for a while the water at the well of sorrow, for no human escapes the pain and hurt of the loss of a beloved. I am not without those feelings. But remember, everything whirls in constant motion. Only nothingness can ever stand still. Transition is all there is.*

"*Don't waste your only life fighting the inevitable, crescendoing crest of human-caused change, when right ahead of the crest still lies enough honey-sweet taste of wild loveliness to season your life with joy."*

The chill autumn breeze tenuously touched my cheek, a soft solicitation to return to the now. Accepting the invitation, I turned slowly to seek the wind's direction and feel the breeze fall full on my face. I thought of his words spoken long ago and recognized grains of truth for me.

For there will long be battles on too many fronts for those who love what is wild. But passion prolonged becomes frenzy; unceasing defense depletes the soul. The heart itself takes its time of rest, beating a balance of give and receive in rhythms of action and pause.

I hear the song of a white-crowned sparrow, a familiar melody that cheers me all winter long. A harrier flies by. I release my spirit and off it soars, teetering away like the beauty in the feathered wings of that bird.

Wind-sculpted snow and Antelope Island.

*Pickleweed and
mudflats.*

*Storm-battered foam
and cobbled
shoreline on
Fremont Island.*

*Storm-ravaged tiger
beetle and other
insects on jagged
salt crystals.*

Seduction

The question "What first attracted you to the lake?" follows me like my shadow on a sunny day.

The answer is easy: Nothing did. I came as a prostitute.

Thinking back, I remember no beautiful scenery luring me there. No eloquent words spring to mind. Put simply, in exchange for money, I agreed to count birds in a place where I seldom considered going when free to go anywhere I chose.

My birding friends said how lucky I was to do something I like—and get paid.

But when that first contract bound me to a stranger and took away all my freedom to roam, resentment dulled the desire to perform.

So, for months I came three times a week, and every time I came, my mind rebelled at the charade and lapsed into mutiny. Like a bird that gets the urge to leave will take wing and fly away, off my thoughts would scamper, to wander somewhere faraway, belligerently refusing to come back or have anything to do with the task. Off my imagination would go, a happy, skipping vagabond leaping over rocky mountain peaks, twirling down shady green forest trails, standing still when awestruck by red sandstone grandeur, or racing a roadrunner back and forth and around in circles until it disappeared into Joshua trees.

Only my body was left behind, shackled by duty, spontaneity dead. Spontaneity's corpse is a depressing load, dullness's invitation to trudge with every step.

I am at a loss as to when it happened. Somewhere between then and now. Gradual and unhurried, as contract led to contract and moments turned into years, that magical lake sent enticements in doses tiny and small. They invited. They tempted and lured.

Each time I came, it seemed a new riddle lay enticingly placed upon the path where my footsteps would come lumbering along.

Oh, how I rose to that challenge. Oh, how I swallowed that bait. For each solution to some puzzle unraveled proved to be a tricky trapdoor that, once opened, suggested that if I kept searching, there was so much more yet to discover.

I had a friend. He was a hermit. He lived by and knew the lake. When he walked there, he mostly walked alone. It was he who taught me much about the pleasures of walking with depth along shores of Great Salt Lake. He detested the shallowness with which our culture approaches the lake. He especially disdained those all-too-common yippy, skippy, straight-line dashes across the lake by those who spew generic words of fill-in-the-blank poetry—words that slide so untouched off the lake that they can be picked up intact and recycled for any and every other landscape.

He once told me he could pinpoint the very moment he first realized I was finally succumbing to the magical enchantment of the lake. It had to do with little mounds and tiger beetles—still to this day two of my favorite lake things. We were mucking our way in ankle-deep mud, counting sandpipers where several small creeks entered the lake. We explored that day in the comfortable stroll known only to those who are friends—like sides of an accordion, we parted, to merge and part again.

He turned to make a comment and unexpectedly found himself alone. Impossible, for in this wide, stretching, flat land of mud, pickleweed, and salt grass, he knew I would have no place to hide.

"I thought you were dead," he boomed, standing above me after finally locating me at some distance, lying motionless on a stretch of damp, salty ground. "What in the world are you doing lying down there for so long?"

"See how the earth is freshly piled into little grainy mounds across these flats? I see them all around the salty shorelines wherever the soil is firm but damp. I'm still trying to figure out what they are."

He knelt and accepted a stiffened salt-grass blade to join with me in brushing earth grains aside to reveal little burrows descending down into the sand.

Rove Beetles.

One mystery solved, but so much more waiting for discovery on that salt playa.

"Look, QUICK!" he said. "There goes a long-legged sprinter, a tiger beetle—the big black one with the markings of tan. Boy, can it ever run. It is ferociously chasing down a brine fly to devour. Tiger beetles are common around the lake, and the larvae are just as predacious as the adults. Here is one of their burrows. See, it is different from the rove beetles' conelike mounds. The soil grains are thrown in a neat pile off to the side. I'll bet there are larvae sitting right near the burrow's top, waiting to grab some unsuspecting insect that chances by."

Through the years, as my haste became increasingly less frantic, and pauses slowly opened a space for curiosity to be, my thoughts slowly ceased their roaming and grew more content to remain on the lake. Acquaintance's harvest was a wild, blissful magic, increasing familiarity with the intricate workings, the glue that gradually bonded me tighter to a lake that has never been easy to know.

Today when I visit the lake, I come body, soul, and mind intact. Spontaneity reigns!

And off I go, body, soul, and mind intact, a happy, skipping vagabond, exploring the mysteries and discovering no end of natural wonders found on Great Salt Lake.

*Common reeds in
late autumn.*

Dried and cracked mud.

Great Salt Lake's Phantom River

On the south shore of Great Salt Lake lies an old river delta, a place filled with magical enchantment, where I wander often, fascinated and spellbound.

It is hard to explain attractions—those magnetisms that draw us to particular places. I suspect seeds planted in my childhood sprouted and blossomed into a mesmerism of such haunting pleasure that it pulls me to the delta.

I spent my childhood on the rather rocky, gravelly soil of an alluvial fan laid down across the Stansbury level of old Lake Bonneville. Elevation 4,445 feet. It was a rural setting then, with a large irrigation canal bordering the mountain side of our property. I roamed freely. There were no fences, and yet I never strayed near that canal. Sometime before my first memory, the dark murky water in that canal took on sinister and spooky characteristics. But when the water left the canal and flowed onto our property to irrigate the fruit trees, it became magical and pleasurable. We were lucky children, for we were allowed to play with abandon in the muddy water.

Today, I cannot watch water in marshes or along waterways that enter the lake, or hear waves lap along the shoreline, without feeling deep stirrings inside. The delta has become a sanctuary, a natural place of quiet solitude, a refuge from the haste of life.

Each new dawn as the sun rises, the delta lies in the shadow of the everlasting hills. I see them to the east as lofty, rigid peaks. The delta *is* the everlasting hills. I kneel and scoop those hills from a natural levee and let grains of sand sift through my fingers.

Saline flats and Antelope Island

Yielding, pliant, flowing. Water and time erode those rigid mountains, carrying them down, bit by bit, to fill the valley below.

Lake Bonneville was no more the beginning than Great Salt Lake is the ending. For over a million years, the site of Great Salt Lake has cradled a series of fresh- and saltwater lakes. The evidence lies layered in up to 12,000 feet of sediment deposited in the deepest graben that underlies the lake.

Rapidly running mountain streams emerge into the valleys, slowing their velocity and selectively dropping larger sediment along the way. Mostly the finer sediments—sand, silt, and clay—reach Great Salt Lake. Much of it is deposited near the river's mouth, forming the deltas as the water flows into the more stationary lake.

I have wandered this delta often and know each meandering curve incised into sediments deposited when the lake was older and higher. I have sat on the bank where the miles-long, meandering bed flares open, and have watched water spread into thousands of acres of channels, cross channels, and around islands, overflowing and seasonally flooding small playas. I have followed the floodplain and splashed along, tracing the curving course of the small, shifting distributaries that form the bird's-foot pattern across the wide delta. I have knelt on levees and watched eddies swirl and floods churn the water to fury. I have lingered on sandbars when the water was low and perched on a river island and felt the power of spring runoff gushing headlong to merge with the salty water of Great Salt Lake.

This magical delta land has puzzled me as much as it has intrigued my imagination. For today it lies dry and deserted, abandoned by the water that once sculpted those intricate patterns into the land. I would occasionally ask people I met there if they knew the answer to this land. One said it was built as a conservation project in the 1930s. He wasn't certain what was being conserved. One thought the pioneers built it in the 1800s. The geologists I asked were unfamiliar with the feature.

Only recently I connected with Don Currey at the University of Utah. About 10,000 years ago, this veritable library of information explained to me, the Jordan River met Great Salt Lake near the Kennecott tailings pond, forming a delta there. Lake Bonneville's gigantic water load depressed the earth's crust into the plastic, molten mantle, and as the water departed, the land rose again. And still rises. This phenomenon, called isostatic rebound, is even greater to the west. Movement along the Wasatch Fault may have contributed. The land where the Jordan River ran 10,000 years ago is tilting. And so the Jordan River has moved its course to the east and north, dallying long enough in this particular spot to sculpt a work of art into the earth. Then it moved on. Dr. Currey told me this place is unique and priceless, one of the last intact river deltas in the country that hasn't been bulldozed.

This special, magical place is the only natural river delta left on Great Salt Lake. So strong is the power of that ancient land sculpture and so little changed in thousands of years that if you stop there and listen carefully, you too will hear the rippling of ghostly waters from out of the past.

*Dew-covered
spider web.*

*Avocets feeding at
sunset.*

Ice floe breakup,
Wasatch Range
and lake fog.

Wind-swept salt patterns on western shore, Strong Knob in the distance.

A Grebe Called Hope

"Did you ever see a grebe fly? Come on, tell me," Dr. Joseph Jehl's staccato voice probed insistently. "You've been to the lake a hundred, perhaps a thousand times. Did you ever see a single grebe fly? Surely you've been there in fall when hundreds of thousands of grebes grace that lake. Now tell me, did you ever, even once, see a single grebe in flight?"

On the wings of memory my thoughts fly west. I relax on the eastern shore of Stansbury Island, feeling the fall breeze chilly and cold. Lulled by the laughter of lake waves, I watch a lone grebe bob up and down, holding the slow rhythm set by the waves. Suddenly, the grebe lurches upward and forward, then downward as it dives, vanishing headfirst into the dark, briny depths. Silently I wait, scanning, expectant till the lake bequeaths the grebe and once again it catches the cadence of the waves. Gone are the bright nuptial colors that paint the grebe in spring. The long golden feathers sun-tinted behind the grebe's ember-red eye have been shed. Gone are the chestnut hues that adorn the sides. Black and white play patterns of dark and light on the body and head of the fall grebe. Sometimes beauty is flamboyant and appreciation comes easily. Sometimes beauty is subtle, seeping slowly into the souls of those who linger long. Some say the fall grebe is drab. To me it is beautiful.

Other memories beckon . . .

The boat zooms north. To the east, the upside-down image of Fremont Island, white with freshly fallen snow, reflects across rolling waves of azure blue water, breaking, the island image into ever-shifting patterns that flow, shimmering and shining, like rivulets of wanton quicksilver. Birds on the water flush and fly. They are not grebes. Mostly gulls. Some grebes frantically dive at our speedy approach. Others hidden amidst a departing splash give only a fleeting glimpse. Sometimes all that is left is a concentric ring of ripples whose center marks the point of grebe submersion.

On Antelope Island, the sinking sun silhouettes thousands of peak-headed birds against glistening wavelets . . .

"You haven't, have you?" Joe's words fetch me back to the room.

One reason you don't see grebes fly is because often in autumn they can't. Species like gulls and phalaropes select small portions of brine shrimp from the lake's buffet. But grebes go gluttonously after the shrimp; they alone pursue the shrimp relentlessly into their underwater domain. Grebes have somehow adapted, for no bird could ingest large quantities of brine and survive. Dr. Jehl thinks it is the eared grebe's huge tongue that squishes the salty water back into the lake, leaving only a mouthful of nutritious shrimp to swallow.

With little competition for so vast a food source and embraced in the security of a watery shield that few predators can breach, the grebes feast and feast and feast until they become so obese they couldn't fly if they tried. They sit out on that lake for months. At the same time, breast muscles necessary for flight begin to atrophy.

Dr. Jehl, director of Hubbs Sea World Research Institute and an authority on salt lakes, has flown unexpectedly to Salt Lake from San Diego and invited me to join him for a day of research. As he works, he occasionally leans down and pulls yet another limp, black-and-white body from a burlap sack and sets it on the rusty metal table.

"But, Joe," I counter, "such enormous numbers of grebes don't breed on the lake, so they must arrive somehow. As winter approaches, the brine shrimp dwindle, and so do most of the grebes. With legs far back on the body to facilitate diving, grebes take so clumsily to the land that I doubt they walk southward in the fall."

"Yes, grebes do fly, but when they fly, they belong to the night."

The grebes somehow sense that the time nears when the lake will lose its fertility. They repeatedly rise up and flap their wings. Fat decreases. Muscles build. Then one night when the darkness summons, the grebes give answer, leaving the waters of Great Salt Lake behind to merge as voyagers with the night sky.

Dr. Jehl lays a grebe on the scale, records the weight, then slowly rotates the bird with palpating fingers. "Broken wing on this one."

Broken legs, broken clavicles, broken necks. Three bags of broken, bruised, smashed grebes now lie at our feet on the hard cement floor. Something went dreadfully wrong one December night high in the sky above the Great Basin. Many thousands of migrating grebes rained down from the heavens, smashing to earth from Holden to Cedar City, concentrating along I-15, where violent collisions with cars added to the grisly toll.

No one knows for certain why it happened. There was a storm that night, with snow and fog, but grebes—sturdy, strong and rugged—have endured many a squall. For some reason, in this storm the grebes sought refuge from the tempest. Disoriented, they forsook the night; confused, the light became their lodestar. In a beguiling, riverlike guise, the rain-wet cement and asphalt, reflecting the lights from street lamps and headlights, may have seduced the sanctuary-seeking grebes.

"Why do you think it was the lights?" I queried. "This doesn't happen often, but once decades ago the literature tells of a similar occurrence in the desert near the Utah-Nevada border, one of the most desolate spots in the West, hardly a glowing nighttime metropolis."

Dr. Jehl paused, scalpel in hand. "No one can say for certain."

When thousands of confused, disoriented grebes are flying above the desert floor, perhaps it takes but a single light, like the sweet song of a siren, to lure thousands of grebes to their deaths.

Dr. Jehl loosened a label stuck to one of the grebe's lobed toes. "Look at this collection date—15 December 1991," he said. "Five days after impact." He slid the scalpel upward, exposing the breast muscles. "This grebe survived the crash. But notice the minute muscle mass—it starved to death."

Some grebes that plummeted to the earth lived through the brutal beating, and with the dawn they could be seen sitting awkwardly around in unnatural places. Many people, not knowing the nature of the grebe, could not understand why the unharmed grebes didn't just fly away like any sensible bird would do. In a surge of concern and caring, many community groups sought to rescue the grebes. Learning that grebes cannot take flight from the ground, they lovingly lifted their bodies from land and set them gently on water.

But complex chemical reactions rearrange atoms, and internal clocks tick with the universe. Every aspect of grebe migration harmonizes with delicate natural cycles, honed to perfection by millions of years, for grebes are one of the oldest bird families on earth. For grebes caught in this storm, the beating pulse of migration had been extinguished.

Dr. Jehl performed autopsies on several hundred grebes released but found dead by 27 December. Most had suffered massive internal injuries. There were indications that some surviving grebes were able to resume migration. However, since hundreds of downed grebes had been banded and not a single band was recovered at Salton Sea after a massive die-off later that winter, Dr. Jehl stated: "Rescue efforts for the downed birds, therefore, were largely ineffectual."

Steve Hedges, a Cedar City wildlife biologist, folded onto my living-room sofa. "One problem," he said, "was that we put them on the sewage ponds, the only unfrozen water in Cedar City. But grebes don't just need water to take off, they also need space. I watched as many a frustrated grebe tried but was unable to clear the surrounding fence." Steve paused and stood silent for a few moments. Then his hand, finger extended, slowly started moving. "But there was at least one grebe that made it over. It circled round and round. And each time it circled, it circled a little higher till at last it cleared the fence."

I watched Steve's hand circle higher and higher, and suddenly, I am there, the fence at my back, jubilantly watching the grebe disappear high into the sky. Perhaps, I think, hope can triumph after all, and a battered and bludgeoned Great Salt Lake, like that single grebe, can rise above its tribulations.

On the wings of that hope, my thoughts spring high to join the grebe.

"FLY! FLY! FLY!

Your wings beat strong, you bird of beauty, you bird of grace.

Fly! Fly! Fly! Fly high! Fly wild! Fly free! Your body has been bruised and broken, but you heal and you live. You have transcended the bonds that would imprison and confine you.

Fly long! Fly joyously! You are my bird of hope for the future of Great Salt Lake.

Leave the day behind, for you must pass through the sunset to rejoin the night.

*Snow-capped Oquirrh
Mountains and clouds
reflected in backwaters.*

A Dalliance with Eternal Flames

There are warm, gentle days on the lake, when the mind yearns for a time of fallowness. When all control of the trail is relinquished, handed over, and entrusted to whim. When the crimson clouds of a firey dawn parent a pleasure to be followed all day like a sunflower faces the sun. With no place needing to be. Just the blissfulness of lingering, however long, wherever you happen to be.

A friend and I perch on adjacent boulders, part of a low, long, black cliff rising from mud flats in the Rozel Hills. Millions of years have passed since these boulders flowed as molten liquid to this spot, glowing and glistening like embers in evening light.

Looking down at the earth beneath our dangling feet, I could almost be convinced that the fire in those rocks never died but fell to the salt flats and was captured by the pickleweed.

Samphire . . . pickleweed . . . salicornia . . . marshfire—different names, same plant.

Marshfire seems most appropriate this September morning—red and orange tingeing here toward purple, flicking there toward yellow, spreading a diffusion of flame-colored loveliness across the gray-and-white salt flats.

Sometimes I don't understand those words that label Great Salt Lake's beauty harsh: Disagreeable to the senses? Unpleasantly coarse and rough? I think they come from mistaken echoes, accuracy checks forgotten. Or expressed when our hasty timing is a mismatch to the lake. I ponder whether my traditional sense of beauty has been effaced by too many days on the lake, and ask my artist friend if he too finds this place incomprehensibly beautiful. Amused, he laughs and tells me that the beauty has fermented my mind, reminding me that I sit here lazily hanging my feet from a volcanic boulder because he lured me there with promises of incomprehensible beauty.

I notice streaks and spots whitening the sides of the black rock where he sits scanning the small spring oasis below. Others besides him have chosen that vantage point. Many suspects: the cinnamon-brown northern harrier that flushed and teetered away from the bulrush hub marking the freshest core of the brackish spring? Great horned owl? Red-tailed hawk? Kestrel?

Probably all and more at some point in time, for the straight-line view from here is a small, salt-grass meadow around the spring where, earlier, a vole scurried away from my footstep.

Last month when my friend came, he told me there were many snowy plovers racing stop-and-go after brine flies. A few avocets, a few least sandpipers. Today only three killdeer race after brine flies. Life changes at these little, slow-moving spring oases that dot the shores of Great Salt Lake. Never is life abundant. The spring below our feet has about the same relevance to birds of the lake as my house has to my city. And where is the infinite wisdom that determines whether that significance is great or small?

The spring is birthed by water flowing decades long confined in earth s hidden passages. The water frolics forth, spreading many directions in newfound freedom. Trickling here and there, the spring s water pursues myriad shallow courses across near-level land to a destination that for all is the same: Great Salt Lake.

On the distant horizon, the shoreline is crystallized white salt deposited by saturated water, contrasting sharply with purple-tinged water beyond. Wine-red-colored bacteria, highly adapted to near-saturation concentrations of salt, dominate this northern compartment of a human-altered lake.

We slide off our perches and scamper down between gigantic boulders, spotted orange with lichens, reminiscent of tiny remnants of that ancient glow, and join the pickleweed on the beach.

Walking amidst pickleweed always makes me feel free, like casting off tight-fitting clothes. Emancipated. Delivered. Unconfined. The land is open. The sky is free. You can deep-breathe the air, and feel the unrestrained soul expand to fill the space.

Pickleweed is a salt-endurance winner. No other rooted plant on the lakeshore can grow in soil so salty. Pickleweed is a pioneer, often the first to invade. Pickleweed inhabits the edge, the frontier, the changing border that defines that vast, expansive, too salty for growth zone. Two species of pickleweed grow on the lake s salty shore, but the one growing where we walk is an annual, the more common, the species that splashes vivid flame across the saline flats in fall.

Satiated and warmed with pleasure to overflowing, we move on, following the sun through the here and the now, traveling old paths and new paths, main roads and side roads where few people go, until at the close of day, we leisurely end far from the dawn, far from home, on the western side of the lake.

Facing west, looking toward the flamboyance of evening s sunset, I am convinced the fire in those rocks never died but was captured in the pickleweed, for there it glows, brilliantly mirrored in that setting sun.

Rain-drenched pickleweed after autumn storm.

*Golden rabbitbrush
and autumn pastels.*

Indian ricegrass and rodent tracks on Strong Knob.

Fiery clouds and reflections.